MY FIRST LOOK AT VEHICLES

THERE ARE TRAINS ALL AROUND THE WORLD

Trains

KATE RIGGS

CREATIVE EDUCATION

Published by Creative Education

P.O. Box 227, Mankato, Minnesota 56002

Creative Education is an imprint of The Creative Company

Designed by Rita Marshall

Photographs by AP / Wide World (Stringer Yurikozyrev), Artemis Images (ATD Group, Inc.),

Gary J. Benson, Susan E. Benson, Steve J. Brown, Corbis (Minnesota Historical Society),

Getty Images (Hulton Archive, The Image Bank, Stone), Anne Gordon, Bruce Leighty,

Dennis Littler

Printed in the United States of America

Library of Congress Cataloging-in-Publication Data

Riggs, Kate. Trains / by Kate Riggs.

p. cm. — (My first look at vehicles)

Includes index.

ISBN-13: 978-1-58341-529-0

1. Railroads—Trains—Juvenile literature. I. Title.

TF 148.R54 2007   625.1—dc22   2006018706

First edition 9 8 7 6 5 4 3 2 1

TRAINS

ALL ABOARD!

A train is a vehicle that cannot go on roads. Trains have to chug along on special railroad tracks. They have loud whistles. The loud whistle tells everyone that a big train is coming!

Some trains carry people. They can take people over mountains. They can take people under the ground. They can even take them under water! Other trains carry things

TRAINS THAT CARRY PEOPLE HAVE MANY WINDOWS

like food or animals. Trains have strong **engines** that make them move.

The engine is in the locomotive. The loco-motive pulls the other cars that are behind it. Without the locomotive, a train could not move.

The biggest steam locomotives
were huge. Each one weighed more
than 80 elephants put together!

STEAM LOCOMOTIVES GIVE OFF STEAM AND SMOKE

The First Trains

The first trains were wooden wagons. They did not have engines. Horses pulled the wagons along a track. The trains were not very fast.

A man in England named George Stephenson wanted to make trains move faster. In 1814, he built a locomotive to pull a train. It burned wood and coal to make energy. Now trains did not need horses to pull them.

The first railroad to go all
the way across the United States
was finished in 1869.

Trains took people to many places. People could even sleep and eat on a train! A famous train called the *Orient Express* was very fancy. It took people on trips across Europe and Asia.

TRAINS AT WORK

Early trains in the U.S. carried food and mail. People liked eating better food from far-away places. They enjoyed getting letters faster, too.

Trains can go up mountains.

They use special wheels

with sharp edges.

Trains today can carry almost anything. They use special **freight cars**. A boxcar looks like a big box. It can carry smaller things inside. A cattle car looks like a boxcar. But it has holes on the sides. Sometimes you can see farm animals through the holes!

A person called an **engineer** drives the train. A railroad **conductor** keeps track of the people and things on the train. He shouts, "All aboard!" when the train is ready to go.

THE ENGINEER CONTROLS THE TRAIN'S SPEED

It's Electric

Today, many cities have special kinds of trains. When people ride trains, they do not need cars. Subways are trains that travel through underground tunnels. Light rail trains are like buses. They run on tracks on the street.

Lots of trains are electric now. This means that they do not burn coal or wood for energy.

The first subway was in
London, England. It started
carrying people in 1863.

SOME TRAINS PULL BIG LOADS ACROSS COUNTRIES

The TGV is an electric train in France. It can go 238 miles (383 km) per hour!

Some trains are fast. Some trains are slow. If you hear a loud whistle, look for the train. Try to figure out what kinds of things the train is carrying!

THE TGV IS THE FASTEST WHEELED TRAIN IN THE WORLD

Hands-on: Shoe Box Trains

Make your own train, then count all the cars!

What You Need

Shoe boxes

Paint or markers

Construction paper

Scissors

Glue or tape

What You Do

1. Use the paint or markers to decorate your shoe boxes like train cars.
2. Cut round "wheels" out of the construction paper. Glue or tape wheels on each box.
3. Line up the boxes. Cut as many strips of paper as you need to connect them. Glue or tape one strip from the back of one box to the front of the next.
4. Pull your train along, and count all the cars!

TRAIN YARDS HAVE HUNDREDS OF TRAIN CARS

INDEX

WORDS TO KNOW

conductor—the person on a train who greets passengers or keeps track of things

engineer—the person who controls how fast the train moves and where it goes

engines—machines that make trains move

freight cars—containers that a train uses to carry things from one place to another

READ MORE

Balkwill, Richard. *The Best Book of Trains*. New York: Kingfisher, 1999.

Brown, Margaret Wise. *Two Little Trains*. New York: HarperCollins, 2001.

O'Brien, Patrick. *Steam, Smoke, and Steel: Back in Time with Trains*. Watertown, Mass.: Charlesbridge Publishing, 2000.

EXPLORE THE WEB

LEGO Recreation Station http://www.lego.com/eng/trains/recreationstation/

Thomas and Friends http://www.thomasandfriends.com/usa/thomas_the_tank_engine_us_website_homepage.html

The Train Era http://www.transitpeople.org/lesson/train.htm